Yisrael Sheli

My Israel: People and Places

יִשְׂרָאֵל שֶׁלִּי

David Singer

We wish to thank Itzik Eshel and Debi M. Rowe

for their help in perfecting this book.

Photo Credits

Photographs by Rabbi Chuck Briskin and Josh Mason-Barkin unless otherwise noted.

Photographs on pages 63, 79 (top) and 82 (top) are reproduced with the permission of Central Zionist Archive

Photograph of Baron Edmond James de Rothschild on page 76 is reproduced with the permission of The Rothschild Archive

Amihays, page 20; Eyal Bartov/Israelimages, page 49 (left); Bettmann/CORBIS, **pages** 11, 26, 39, 83, (bottom); David Bleicher, page 59; Yehuda Boltshauser, page 89; Bornshtein, page 79 (bottom); Aron Brand, page 37 (center); Corky Buczyk, page 88; Roberto Cerruti, page 56 (top); Ludmilla Cherniak, page 55, Jose Elias da Silva Neto, page 23, (foreground); Francesco Dazzi, page 28; Tzur (Tsuf)Delly, pages 16 (top), 49 (right); Dejan Gileski, pages 21, 73; Patrick Girouard, page 65; Government Office/Israelimages, page 13; Joshua Haviv, page 31; Hanan Isachar/Israelimages, pages 16 (middle and bottom), 36, 58, 61, 74, 90; Israel Ministry of Tourism, page 34; Eugene Ivanov, page 38 (background); Vladimir Khirman, page 9 (top); Michal Levit/Israelimages, page 32 (foreground); Nir Levy, page 37 (right); Liane M, page 55; Andrei Marincas, page 5 (bottom); Itsik Marom/Israelimages, page 64 (bottom); Yasha Mazur/Israelimages, 64, (top); Eoghan McNally, page 91; Mordechai Meiri, page 40; George Muresan, page 24 (bottom); NASA/Israelimages, page 14; Richard Nowitz/Israelimages, pages 41, 43, 92; OPIS, page 52 (bottom); Paul Prescott, pages 23 (background), 24 (top and middle); 32 (background); Lev Radin, page 78; Ya'akov Sa'ar/GPO/Gettyimages, page 33; Sakala, page 80 (bottom); Elisei Shafer, page 19; Moshe Shai/Israelimages, pages 56 (bottom), 77, 86; Josef F.Stuefer, page 10 (background); Ruthie Talby/Israelimages, page 12 (bottom); Israel Talby/Israelimages, pages 27, 67; John Theodor/Photozion, pages 18, 50 (top), 85 (top); Kheng Guan Toh, page 5 (top); Christine Tripp, pages 6, 71; Marc Van Vuren, pages 51 (background), 52 (top); Birute Vijeikiene, page 29; VojtechVik, page 22; Peter M.Wilson/CORBIS, page 60; Stavchansky Yalov, page 51 (foreground); Arkady Yarmolenko, page 81; Lane Yerkes, page 72; Ron Zimri, page 9 (bottom); Vladimir Zivkovic, page 17.

ISBN 10: 1-934527-25-4

ISBN 13: 978-1-934527-25-2

Torah Aura Productions • 4423 Fruitland Avenue, Los Angeles, CA 90058

(800) BE-Torah • (800) 238-6724 • (323) 585-7312 • fax (323) 585-0327

E-MAIL <misrad@torahaura.com> • Visit the Torah Aura website at www.torahaura.com

MANUFACTURED IN MALAYSIA

TABLE OF CONTENTS

FINDING ISRAEL

Where in the world is Israel?
Can you find it on a globe?
Look at the map below.

Israel is in the middle where three continents meet: Africa, Asia, and Europe. Before there were airplanes, many travelers passed through Israel on their way from one place to another.

Many of the people who came through Israel were from countries who wanted to control Israel. Some of them conquered Israel for themselves. The Greeks, Babylonians, Romans, Byzantines, Arabs, Christians, and Ottomans are just some of the peoples that controlled and lived in Israel at one time or another.

So many different people in such a small place!

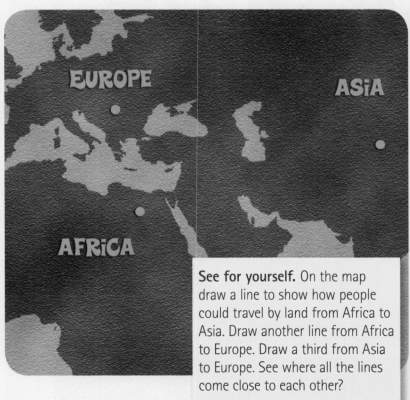

See for yourself. On the map draw a line to show how people could travel by land from Africa to Asia. Draw another line from Africa to Europe. Draw a third from Asia to Europe. See where all the lines come close to each other?

ABRAHAM AND SARAH

CHAPTER 1: ISRAEL

Every story has a beginning.

The story of Israel starts with the story of Abraham and Sarah, the first Jews.

Thousands of years ago, Abraham and Sarah lived in the land of Ur. Ur is far to the northeast of the Land of Israel. Abraham was like everyone else. But one day something special happened. God spoke to Abraham. God said: "Go from your land, from where you were born, from your father's house, and go to the land that I will show you" (Genesis 12:1). God made a promise: "I will make you a great nation, and I will bless you. I will make your name great. You shall be a blessing" (Genesis 12:2). Abraham agreed to leave his home. God led Abraham and Sarah to the Land of Israel.

Why do you think Abraham decided to go? Abraham left his home in Ur without asking God any questions. He didn't even know where he was going, but he went anyway. How do you think Abraham felt when God spoke to him? What do you think Abraham was thinking? Why did Abraham leave his home to go to a brand new place?

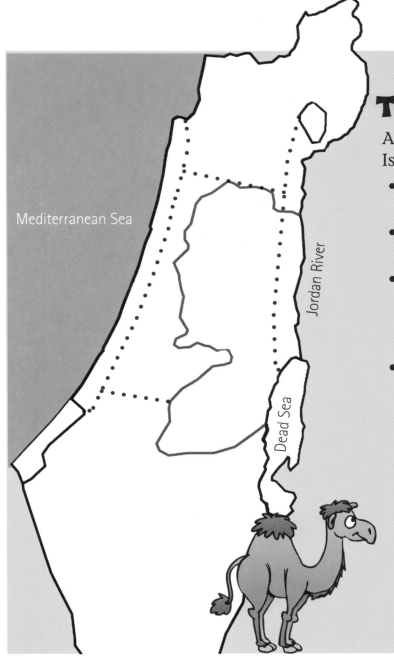

Mediterranean Sea

Jordan River

Dead Sea

THE LAND OF ISRAEL

Abraham came to the Land of Israel. Israel has many different areas:

- The north is very green with plants and trees. It is called the *Galil*.

- The south is a very big desert called the *Negev*.

- In the middle of Israel, the east is very hilly. The west is flat. Most Israelis live here, along the coast. This is the *coastal plain*.

- Israel has two large lakes: The *Kinneret* in the north and the *Dead Sea* in the south. The Jordan River connects them. This is the *Jordan River Valley*.

Fill in the Map

Look at the outline of Israel to the left. Do you remember the four different areas of the country? What makes them different?

Color in the map of Israel to show the four different areas we've learned about. Then label each area.

Jacob

Jacob was the grandson of Abraham. He was the son of Isaac and Rebekkah. One night, Jacob encountered an angel. The two wrestled all night. As the sun began to rise, the angel begged Jacob to let him go. But Jacob said, "I WILL NOT LET YOU GO UNLESS YOU BLESS ME."

The angel gave Jacob a special blessing–a new name. The angel named Jacob: "Israel." Israel means "one who struggles with God." That is the origin of the name of Israel. It is also why Jews are sometimes called B'nai Yisrael. Jews are the families of Israel.

NEGEV

Makhtesh Ramon is a giant crater. It formed over millions of years as water carved out the crater. From the top, you can see an incredible view of the Negev Desert. ▼

Did you know that almost two-thirds of Israel is desert? This area is called the Negev, which comes from the Hebrew root meaning "dry."

For most of his life, Jacob lived in the Land of Israel, in places near the north of the Negev Desert, such as Beersheva.

The Negev Desert is very dry. It gets almost no rain ever. Most of the Negev is filled with rocks: big rocks and little rocks and lots of sand. There are very few plants and some camels. Even though it is a really dry place, Israelis have found ways to grow plants and food in the desert. They work hard to make the desert bloom.

MAKING THE DESERT BLOOM

Plants need freshwater. Saltwater kills plants. There is not much water in the Negev. Israel has invented machines to take the salt out of seawater. Israel leads the world in desalination (taking salt out of seawater) technology.

Connect the pipes to get this freshwater from the desalination plant to the orange trees in the kibbutz field.

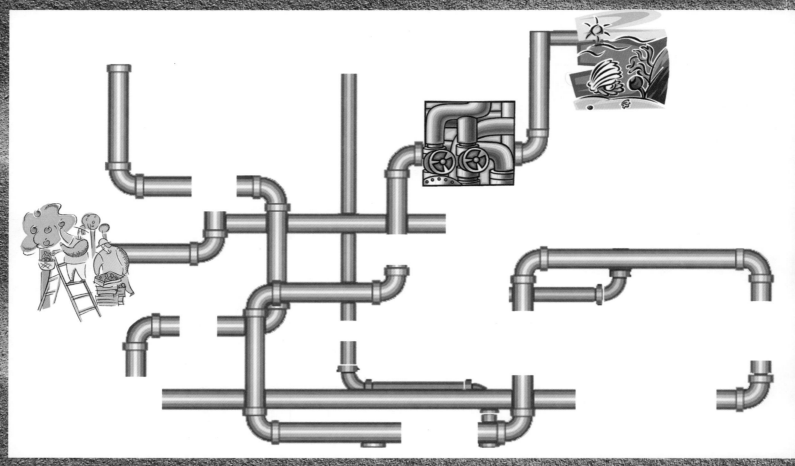

CHAPTER 3: SDE BOKER

David Ben Gurion

Israelis call David Ben Gurion the "father of Israel." David Ben Gurion was the first prime minister of Israel. He was the leader who helped Israel gain independence in 1948. Ben Gurion was also just a regular man. He had big messy hair and was very short. Every morning he liked to go to the beach in Tel Aviv to swim and exercise. He liked to do headstands, too!

David Ben Gurion loved the desert. He thought it was really important for Jews to move there and make the desert bloom. With enough hard work, Israelis found ways to have parks, schools, and even farms in the middle of the desert. To show Israelis just how important it was to settle the desert, he moved there with his wife. They left their apartment behind in Tel Aviv and moved a to a kibbutz in the Negev.

Today, David Ben Gurion and his wife are buried in Kibbutz Sde Boker. From his grave, you can look out at the Negev Desert that Ben Gurion loved so much.

When you visit Sde Boker, you can come and pay your respects to David Ben Gurion. His grave is a national monument. Many people visit it every year to learn about this great Jewish hero and the things he did in his life.

Sde Boker is a lovely kibbutz in the middle of the desert. It overlooks a huge crater down below. You can go on hikes in the crater through dried up riverbeds. Sometimes you can see ibex and other animals. It's not an easy hike, and the desert gets very hot, so be sure to bring a hat and plenty of water!

WHAT'S in a Name?

David Ben Gurion's last name wasn't always Ben Gurion. In fact, when he was born his name was David Green. How did it change? When he came to Israel, David wanted to have a name that sounded more Jewish and more Israeli. So he changed his name a little to sound more like a name in the Torah. From Green, he changed it to Ben (son of) Gurion, which sounds a lot like Green.

What is your Hebrew name? Lots of people have Hebrew names that are very similar to their English names. Is yours?

Write out your Hebrew name here.

_____

_____

13

Ilan Ramon

Ilan Ramon was Israel's first astronaut and one of only a few Jewish astronauts ever! In 2003, he joined NASA astronauts in the Space Shuttle *Columbia* and blasted into space for two weeks.

It was really important to Ilan to bring some things into space with him that would celebrate his Jewishness. Both his mother and grandmother were survivors of the Holocaust. He brought a drawing by a fourteen-year-old boy named Petr Ginz who had died in the *Shoah*. The drawing was a picture of the earth from the view of someone standing on the moon. Ilan also brought with him a miniature copy of the Torah!

When the Space Shuttle Columbia was returning to Earth on February 1, 2003, a tragedy happened. When Columbia was coming back towards Earth, it overheated and crashed over Texas, killing all the astronauts onboard.

Ilan Ramon was awarded the Congressional Space Medal of Honor. He is remembered as a hero and role model to Israelis and Jews everywhere.

BEERSHEVA

▼ Abraham's well

Ilan Ramon lived in the Israeli city Beersheva.

In the Torah, Beersheva is mentioned many times. Abraham, Isaac, and Jacob all went there. Beersheva is in the very north of the Negev Desert, so it has always been a place that people pass through on their way into the wilderness. Even today, it is hard to drive into the Negev without passing through or near Beersheva. It is called the "Gateway to the Negev."

Today, Beersheva is one of Israel's largest cities. There are many things to do in Beersheva. Beersheva is probably best known for the Ben Gurion University. Ben Gurion University is a very large school. People come to study at Ben Gurion from all around Israel and all over the world. Many American students come to Ben Gurion to learn Hebrew or to continue their college learning in Israel.

▲ Ben Gurion University

JEWS iN SPACE

Being in space created lots of questions for Ilan Ramon about how to be Jewish. He spoke with some rabbis to figure out how to be Jewish while in the space shuttle.

Can you think of some problems related to being Jewish that could have come up? Look at the activities below. There are problems in space with each one. Think of what the problem is and then describe a possible way to fix it.

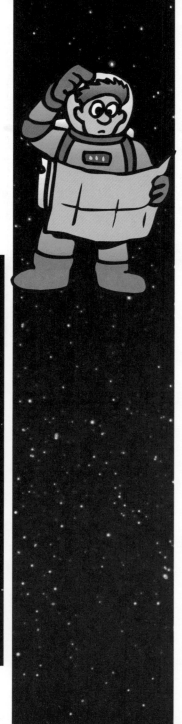

16

King Solomon

King Solomon was the son of King David. He was known for being a very wise person. Jews from all over came to seek his advice.

Once, two women came before King Solomon. They both claimed that a baby was theirs.

"It's my baby," said the first women.

"No, it's my baby!" said the second.

King Solomon thought long and hard, until finally he had an answer.

"I will make both of you happy," he said. "Cut the baby in half, and each of you can have half." This was his solution.

"No!" cried the first woman. "I would rather she have my child than him being hurt!"

And, with that, King Solomon knew that the first woman was the true mother. The mystery was solved.

How did King Solomon know who was the real mother? Can you think of a situation in your life in which King Solomon's wisdom could help solve a big problem?

King Solomon helped to strengthen the Israelite Kingdom. He built a Temple in Jerusalem and unified B'nai Yisrael.

Eilat

In the very south of Israel, on the coast of the Red Sea, King Solomon built a settlement named Eilat. Here, he built fleets of ships to help defend his kingdom.

Today, in the same area as King Solomon's Eilat is the modern city of Eilat. Eilat is in the Negev Desert and very far from most other cities.

Eilat is the only place in Israel that is on the Red Sea. It has a big port for shipping things around the world. From Eilat you can see Jordan, Egypt, and even Saudi Arabia! Eilat is best known as a fun place to go on vacation. Eilat has beautiful beaches with big, fancy hotels up and down the coast.

The weather is always perfect in Eilat, assuming you like it hot! It is very hot in Eilat almost all year long. Tourists come to Eilat to sit on the beach and sunbathe. Eilat is a perfect place to rest and relax. It is also well known as a place to go snorkeling. The sea near Eilat is filled with coral reefs and lots of colorful fish.

Snorkeling

Count the number of fish you can see in this picture from Eilat.

Josephus was a Jewish governor in the Galilee during Roman times. In the year 66 C.E., the Jews revolted against the Romans. When Josephus was captured by the Romans, he decided to join them.

Josephus became a historian. He wrote many books. One book he wrote was called *The History of the Jews*. This book told the history of the Jewish people from the time of Creation. Josephus wrote another book called *The War of the Jews*. This book tells the story of the Jewish revolt against the Romans.

CHAPTER 6: MASADA

Masada was a fortress built in the Judean Desert, above the Dead Sea. After destroying Jerusalem in 70 C.E., the Romans chased some zealots (Jewish revolutionaries) to Masada. The zealots took over the fortress and defended it as the last place in Israel not conquered by Rome. The Roman army arrived in 72 C.E. Because the fortress is on top of such steep cliffs, the zealots were able to defend themselves against the huge Roman army for a whole year!

The Romans built a ramp up to the top of Masada so that they could conquer the mountain. The Jewish zealots knew that they could not win a fight. They knew the Romans would capture them and send them into slavery. On the night before the approaching Roman invasion, they chose to take their own lives instead of being captured. When the Roman soldiers finally got inside Masada, not a single person was left alive.

MASADA

When you visit Masada, there are lots of things to see and learn. The fortress is filled with fancy baths and other buildings, just like a modern spa! You can walk inside the remains of the baths and even parts of a palace. When the Jews lived on Masada they even built a synagogue. There are great spots on Masada where you can look out and see down to the Dead Sea.

On the scroll make a list of Jewish things that are worth protecting.

WHaT WOULD YOU FiGHT FOr?

The Jewish zealots of Masada made a hard choice. They decided that they cared so much about their freedom to be Jews and not become slaves that they would not give in to the Romans. Josephus wrote about Eliezer, the zealot leader, and his speech about how important Judaism was to him and his followers.

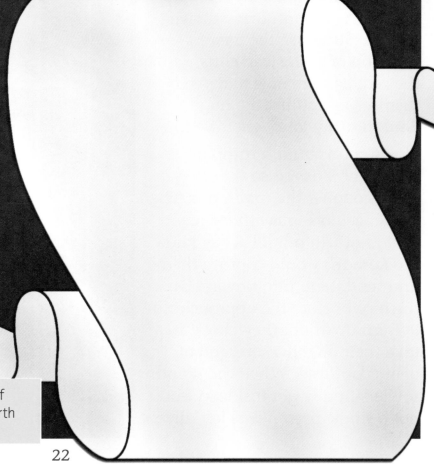

CHAPTER 7: EIN GEDI

KING DAVID

Ein Gedi is a place King David visited.

Just at the edge of Jerusalem, the hills slope steeply towards the desert. Jerusalem is thousands of feet above sea level, but only a few miles to the east, the desert is more than a thousand feet below sea level. This is the lowest place on Earth!

The Judean Desert gets almost no rain. Nothing grows there, and all you can see is lots and lots of bare earth and stones. But there, in the middle of the desert, in between two hills, you can find the oasis Ein Gedi.

When David was a boy he defeated Goliath with his sling. He became the harpist to King Saul, the first king of Israel. He grew up to be a great general. Saul grew jealous of David and tried to kill him. David ran away. He went to Ein Gedi. Saul chased him there. David hid in a cave and escaped. After Saul was killed in battle, David became the next king of Israel. The Bible tells us that David used his harp to write the Psalms.

EiN GEDi TODAY

Lots of people come to visit Ein Gedi every day. You can take a small hike into the oasis. Soon you are surrounded by lots of plants and flowers and birds.

At the end of the hike is a giant waterfall and pool of water. It's fun to splash around in the water to cool off!

WHaT'S an OaSiS?

An oasis is a place in the middle of the desert where trees grow and animals live. But animals and plants need water to live! Where does the water come from?

When rain falls in the Judean hills around Jerusalem, some of it goes into the ground. Gravity makes the water fall through the rocks. Some of it finds its way underground into the desert, where it comes back out of the rocks in the form of small rivers and waterfalls.

This is what happens at Ein Gedi. Even though it almost never rains there, Ein Gedi's water source flows constantly. The spring gives life to birds and ibex as well as lots of plants. Ein Gedi is an important nature reserve in Israel.

Ibex ▶

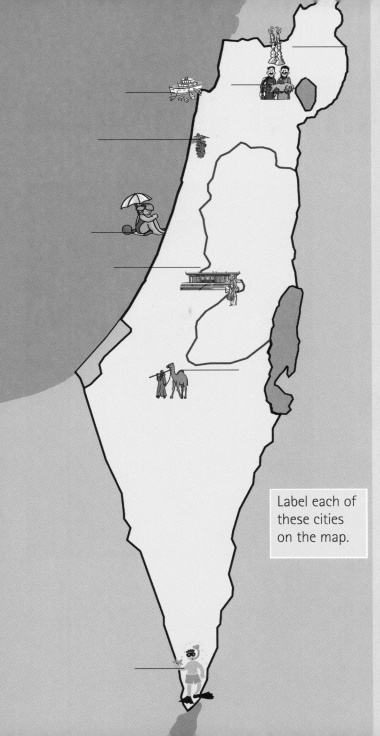

Twelve Tribes

King David was the first person to unite B'nai Yisrael into one large kingdom. King David brought together the twelve tribes, and built his capital in Jerusalem.

Before King David, each of the twelve tribes lived in a different part of Israel. The map of Israel was divided, based on which tribe lived in each area.

Today, Israel's map is divided by the different cities around the country. In the north are Haifa, Tzfat, and T'veria. In the middle are Tel Aviv, Zikhron Ya'akov, and Jerusalem. In the south are Be'ersheva and Eilat.

Label each of these cities on the map.

Tel Aviv

Be'ersheva

Tzfat

Zikhron Ya'akov

Haifa

T'veria

Eilat

Jerusalem

25

CHAPTER 8: THE OLD CITY OF JERUSALEM

MOSHE Dayan

Moshe Dayan was a military leader of Israel. He was best recognized by the patch he wore over his left eye. He led Israel in many of its wars. During the Six Day War of 1967, Moshe Dayan led the capture of the Old City of Jerusalem.

For the first time in two thousand years, Jerusalem was the united capital of the Jewish people. Jews from all over Israel rushed to Jerusalem to come to the Old City for the first time in twenty years. Thanks to Moshe Dayan, Jews could finally come back to the Old City and the *Kotel* inside of it.

THE OLD CITY

The Old City is divided into four quarters: the Muslim Quarter, the Christian Quarter, the Jewish Quarter, and the Armenian Quarter.

The Jewish Quarter is where the *Kotel* is. Lots of Jews live in the Jewish Quarter, and there are many *yeshivot* there, too. In the middle is a giant square with a park and many restaurants and shops. It's a great place to eat falafel or have a drink during a busy day of touring!

The Muslim Quarter is a very important place to Muslims around the world. In fact, Muslims consider Jerusalem one of their holy cities, just like Jews and Christians. In the same place where the Temple once stood, on the Temple Mount, there are two giant mosques. One mosque, called the Dome of the Rock, is a beautiful building with a giant gold dome on top. All day long, as the sun shines on the golden dome, it sparkles and shines. Because it is so big, the Dome of the Rock can be seen from many places throughout Jerusalem. The mosque is built on top of the spot where Abraham almost sacrificed Isaac. The second mosque is called Al Aqsa. Muslims believe that this mosque stands on the spot where their prophet, Mohammed, ascended to heaven. It is a very holy and important place to Muslims. Thousands of Muslims come to the Temple Mount to pray every day.

Not far from the Temple Mount and the *Kotel* is a very important place for Christians. In the Christian Quarter is the Church of the Holy Sepulcher. This is one of the most important churches in Christianity. The Church of the Holy Sepulcher is a very old place. Different parts of the church were built at different times, but some of them are hundreds and hundreds of years old. The church is very dark, and filled with candles that visitors can light. As you walk through the church's halls, you can smell incense.

CENTER OF THE WORLD

Did you know that Jerusalem was such an important place to these three different religions? For this reason, Jerusalem has sometimes been seen as the very center of the world. Old maps often were drawn with Jerusalem at the middle.

Even though the city is unified as part of the capital of Israel, Jerusalem is special to billions of people around the world. Israel works hard to make sure that all religions and religious sites are protected in the city so everyone can pray in the place which is special to them.

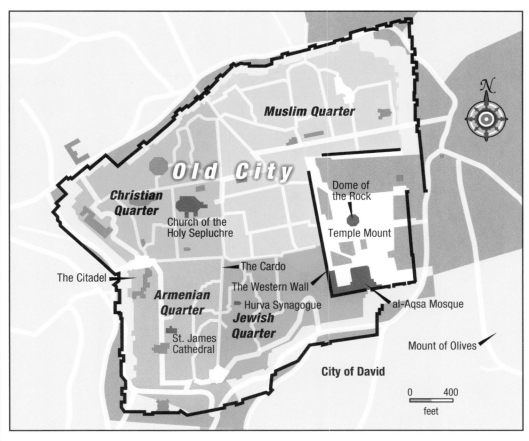

In What Quarter Is Each of the Following Sites?

_____ Hurva Synagogue

_____ Dome of the Rock

_____ Church of the Holy Sepulchre

_____ The Citadel

_____ David's City

_____ The Cardo

_____ al-Aqsa Mosque

_____ St. James Cathedral

_____ The Western Wall

29

CHAPTER 9: THE KOTEL

EZRA

Ezra was an important leader of ancient Israel. He led B'nai Yisrael back to the Land of Israel after being in exile in Babylonia.

Ezra was a scribe. The Torah was very important to him. He was sad that many of the people had never heard of the Torah. So what did he do? He brought them all together at a gate in Jerusalem and read to them the entire Torah!

When Ezra brought the people back to Jerusalem, the Holy Temple was in ruins. B'nai Yisrael began a project of building the Second Temple on Mount Moriah—the exact same place where we remember that Abraham almost sacrificed Isaac.

The Temple was the center of the lives of the Jewish people. There, they brought sacrifices and other gifts for God. The Temple was seen as God's home on Earth. The Temple was so special and holy that people felt God's presence there.

Is there a place that is special and holy to you? Where do you feel God's presence?

WHAT'S IN A NAME?

The Temple was destroyed first by the Babylonians. It was rebuilt, and then destroyed again by the Romans. All that is left is one wall that held up the hill on which the Temple stood.

Over time, that wall has had many names: the Wailing Wall, the Western Wall, and, simply, *Ha-Kotel* (Hebrew for "the Wall").

Most people stopped calling it the Wailing Wall after 1967. In that year Israel reunited the whole city of Jerusalem and, for the first time in a long while, Jews were allowed to visit *Ha-Kotel*.

Why do you think the wall was called "wailing" in the first place? Why might you or might you not call it "wailing" today?

TODAY

Jews all around the world have dreamed for thousands of years of being able to visit *Ha-Kotel* . Now we can.

In front of the wall is a giant plaza. In the back of the plaza are lots of Israeli flags. But as you walk towards the front of the plaza, all you see is the giant wall of the Temple in front of you. The stones are huge. Some of them weigh thousands of pounds.

31

Notes in the Wall

One Jewish tradition is to place prayers inside the cracks in *Ha-Kotel*. Jews from all over the world come to Israel and write down prayers to God on pieces of paper that they stuff in between the giant stones. Sometimes the wall is overflowing with people's prayers!

One day, when you get to visit *Ha-Kotel*, you will be able to write your own special prayer. Imagine that you are there now.

Use this space to write your own special note to God.

▼View of *ha-Kotel* and the plaza.

TEDDY KOLLEK

Jerusalem is an old city. King David made Jerusalem his capital. King Solomon built the Temple there. Eliezer Ben Yehudah lived in Jerusalem when he was making up new Hebrew words. Yehudah Amichai wrote poems about the Old City of Jerusalem. But Jerusalem is also a very new city. It has big, tall buildings and coffee shops and even new trains that run on the street to zip people around town. One person who helped to make that happen was Teddy Kollek.

Teddy Kollek was once the mayor of Jerusalem. He was liked so much that he was elected five times! He was Jerusalem's mayor for twenty-eight years. It was very important to him to make Jerusalem into a great modern city. He helped to build lots of cultural buildings as well as parks and schools throughout the city.

In the south part of Jerusalem is a giant soccer stadium named after Teddy Kollek. Israelis love the game of soccer. One of the country's favorite soccer teams is called Beitar Jerusalem. Their home field is Teddy Kollek Stadium. Ha-Poel Jerusalem is another soccer team that plays there.

MODERN CITY OF JERUSALEM

One of Teddy Kollek's nicknames is *Avi ha-Muze'on*, the father of the museum. He helped to build the Israel Museum, Israel's main national museum. This is where Israel puts all of the most important artifacts for safekeeping.

The museum has lots of different exhibits. Some show off great works of art. Others have old Jewish objects like kiddush cups and Torah covers. The museum even has two whole synagogues from Europe and Asia inside of it!

The Israel Museum is best known for one of its buildings that looks like a giant Hershey's kiss. This building is called the Shrine of the Book. Inside are kept lots of really old Hebrew scrolls. The scrolls were found in caves in the desert, near the Dead Sea. These scrolls have books of the Bible that are two thousand years old! They are some of the oldest copies of the Bible that have ever been found.

Be an ARCHitect

When the Dead Sea Scrolls were found, they were inside small clay pots hidden in the desert. All those clay pots had lids. The Shrine of the Book was designed to look like one of those lids!

How would you design The Shrine of the Book? Would you make it look like the pot lid?

Use this space to draw your own building for the Dead Sea Scrolls.

"if you will it, it is no Dream."

THEODOR HERZL

Theodor Herzl grew up in Europe a little more than a hundred years ago. He was angry that Jews were not always treated equally and was sad there was no country that Jews could call their own.

Theodor Herzl decided that the best thing that could happen would be for the Jewish people to build their own country. He wrote down his ideas in a book called *The Jewish State*. At the time he wrote his book, Jews were scattered all over the world.

He wanted to change all that. He wanted Jews to live together in one country. He then wrote a novel, *Altneuland* (in English, *The Old New Land;* in Hebrew, *Tel Aviv*).

Have you ever wanted to do something but been scared because it seemed like it would be too hard? What was it? How did that feel?

Herzl wasn't scared of trying to do something really hard. Lots of people told him there was no way he could make it happen, but Herzl was sure he could. He said "If you will it, it is no dream."

In the west of Jerusalem, on top of the tallest hill in the city, is Herzl's grave. The hill is called Mount Herzl. It is named after him because Herzl is seen as the "founding father" of modern Israel.

Mount Herzl is Israel's national cemetery. It is where all the leaders of the country and lots of soldiers are buried when they die.

Mount Herzl is a peaceful place with lots of trees and plants. It is a sad place, because lots of people are buried there, but it is also a happy place because it is proof that Theodor Herzl's idea came to life.

MOUNT HERZL

▲ The Israeli Military Cemetery is on Mount Herzl. The Israeli army is called צהל *Tzahal*, the Israeli Defense Force. Most Israelis—men and women—serve in the army right after high school, and some make a career out of the army.

THE FLAG

Israel's flag is blue and white. It has two large blue stripes and a blue Star of David (*Magen David*) in the middle.

Try to think why the flag looks like this. What does the Star of David stand for? What might the two stripes mean? Does Israel's flag look like any other Jewish items that you know about?

If you were going to make your own flag of Israel, what would it look like? What symbols and colors will you choose?

Golda Meir moved with her family to the United States when she was eight. They lived in Milwaukee, Wisconsin. In school, Golda loved to help out her classmates and organize to fight for what was right. She helped raise money to buy textbooks for class and created a Zionist group for her friends.

As she grew up, Golda became more and more excited by the idea of helping to build a Jewish state. She loved the idea of Jews having their own country in Israel. When she finished school, she got married and moved with her new husband to the Land of Israel.

Golda Meir was always a leader in Israel. She was involved with helping to build the state and was even one of the people who signed Israel's Declaration of Independence. She served in Israel's government as a parliament member for almost twenty years.

In 1969, she became the prime minister. She was the first woman prime minister of Israel! Only a few countries in the world have ever had a woman president or prime minister. Israel was one of the first.

THE KNESSET

The Knesset is Israel's parliament. It meets in a giant building on top of a hill in the middle of Jerusalem. The Knesset is where Israel's leaders meet, enact laws, and discuss the future of the Jewish state. The Knesset is known for being a place where politicians like to argue about the best way to improve Israel.

40

Outside of the Knesset is a giant menorah. The menorah, which stands in the area in front of the Knesset gates, was designed by the Jewish-English sculptor Benno Elkan. It was donated to the Knesset by the members of the British Parliament on April 15, 1956. The menorah has always been a symbol of the Jewish people. It is the official emblem of Israel. The menorah outside of the Knesset has pictures on all of its branches, showing important people and events in Jewish history.

List three moments in Jewish history that you would put on the menorah.

1. _____

2. _____

3. _____

THE KNESSET MENORAH

Eliezer Ben Yehudah

Do you know where Hebrew comes from? Hebrew is the language of the Torah. Hebrew has been the language of Jewish prayer for thousands of years, too. But for most of Jewish history, Jews didn't actually speak Hebrew. Hebrew was known as *Lashon ha-Kodesh*—the holy language. Hebrew was used only in the Torah and important religious documents. For everyday talk, Jews spoke the language of the place they lived.

When Jews started moving back to Israel over a hundred years ago, they had a huge problem—they couldn't understand each other! They spoke German and Russian, Arabic, Yiddish, and lots of other languages.

Eliezer ben Yehudah wanted to fix this problem. He thought it was very important that Hebrew be turned into a modern language that all Jews could speak. So what did he do? He learned the Hebrew of the Torah, and started speaking it. He and his wife spoke only in Hebrew. When they didn't know a word for something, they'd point to it and make up a new word!

Thanks to the work of Eliezer ben Yehudah, Hebrew is now a modern spoken language. Millions of people all around the world speak Hebrew. It is the language that connects all Jews no matter where they live.

MIDRAHOV

One of the coolest places in Jerusalem is named after Eliezer ben Yehudah, just down the street from where he lived.

Ben Yehudah Street is a big outdoor mall in the center of the city where no cars are allowed. Lots of restaurants sell falafel and shwarma and other delicious Israeli foods. Ben Yehudah Street has lots of stores that sell Jewish items like *tallitot* and *hannukiyot*. There are also many musicians who perform there. Every day, Ben Yehudah Street is filled with lots of people eating, drinking and having a good time in Jerusalem.

The Hebrew word *Rehov* means "street." This pedestrian mall is called the Midrahov from the same root, רחב, that means "wide."

MAHANEH YEHUDAH

Nearby is the Mahaneh Yehudah Market. Another name for this market is the shuk. The shuk is Jerusalem's big outdoor market. Almost every type of food is sold here—lots of fresh vegetables, fish, meats, nuts, and snacks. It's loud and crowded and lots of fun!

Mahaneh Yehudah is the most fun on Friday afternoons. The alleys and shops fill with people trying to buy food before Shabbat. Everything smells delicious and people's faces are filled with smiles as they get ready for Shabbat.

SHOPPING IN THE *MIDRAHOV*

The *Midrahov* is a great place to shop. Pick one T-shirt to buy. Pick one kippah to buy. And pick one piece of jewelry to buy.

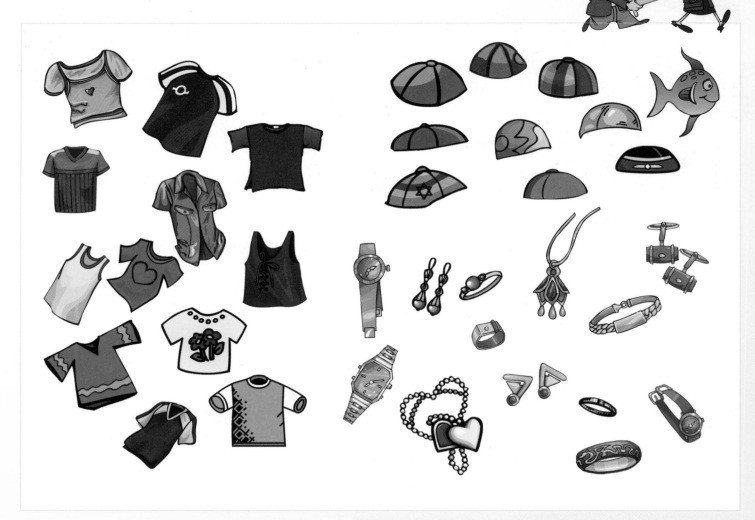

Hannah Szenez

About eighty years ago, Hannah Szenez (pronounced Shenesh) was living in Israel. She was born in Hungary, and came to Israel when she was a teenager. She lived on a kibbutz where she spent most of her time working in the fields.

When World War II and the *Shoah* began, she decided to do what she could to help the Jews still living in Hungary. She trained to be a paratrooper in the British army. She left her friends behind to fight to save the lives of Jews.

Hannah Szenez was captured while fighting in Europe. She is considered a hero in Israel, and her story is a symbol of the heroes of the *Shoah*. Hannah Szenez was not just a paratrooper. When she lived on the kibbutz in Israel, Hannah was a poet. Her most famous poem is "Eli Eli." It describes the things in life that she found most beautiful.

> My God, My God, I pray that these things never end,
> The sand and the sea,
> The rush of the waters,
> The crash of the Heavens,
> The prayer of the heart.

YAD VASHEM

Just down the hill from Theodor Herzl's grave, at the bottom of Mount Herzl, is Yad Vashem, Israel's memorial to the Holocaust. In Hebrew, the word for the Holocaust is *Shoah*. Yad Vashem teaches people about what happened during the *Shoah*.

<u>H</u>annah Szenez was just one of lots of people whose story is told at Yad Vashem.

Do you know someone who lived during the *Shoah*? Think of ways that you can share their story.

Yad Vashem has many different parts to it. In the center is a museum that teaches about the history of the *Shoah*. There are pictures and movies and artifacts to look at and learn from. Next to the museum is a school. Groups can come and learn more about the *Shoah*. Every day, survivors come and share their stories with the younger generation.

Yad Vashem is a very big place. Throughout the grounds, there are statues and artwork dedicated to those who died in the *Shoah*. There are special trees planted in Yad Vashem's "Avenue of the Righteous". Each tree is dedicated to a "Righteous Gentile," a non-Jew who helped Jews during the *Shoah*. The Righteous Gentiles helped to save thousands of Jews from the Nazis. Each is thanked with a tree planted in his or her name at Yad Vashem.

PRAYER OF THE HEART

There are many ways to honor the people who died during the *Shoah*. One way is to learn about what happened to them and make sure it never happens again to anyone in the world. Another way is to tell their story to other people.

Design your own sculpture for a Holocaust memorial.

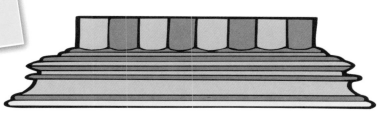

CHAPTER 15: MODI'IN

Judah Maccabee

Hundreds of years after the Temple was rebuilt in Jerusalem, the Land of Israel was conquered by Greeks. They made the Temple unholy and made rules to keep Jews from living a Jewish life. Even Torah study was outlawed!

Judah Maccabee led a revolt to gain freedom for the Jews. Does this story sound familiar? If so, that's because we celebrate Judah Maccabee's victory against the Greeks every year at <u>H</u>anukkah! The story we tell every year is that when the Maccabee took back the Temple in Jerusalem, they found only enough oil for the menorah to last one day. But the menorah was supposed to be lit every day, and new supplies were eight days away!

We remember a great miracle where the oil lasted all eight days until new oil arrived. We celebrate this every year by lighting the <u>h</u>annukiyah and eating latkes!

MODI'IN

Reconstruction of Modi'in in the time of the Maccabees.

Judah Maccabee and his followers lived at the base of the Judean hills, very close to Jerusalem. Today there is a modern town of Modi'in, almost exactly between Tel Aviv and Jerusalem, in the middle of Israel.

Unlike Jerusalem, Modi'in is a very new city. The first building was built there in 1993. Compare that to buildings in Jerusalem which are thousands of years old!

Modi'in is one of the biggest cities in Israel. It has schools and houses and lots of parks. A lot of Americans who make aliyah choose to live in Modi'in. Can you think of why?

Do you know how old your city is? Are there lots of old places to visit, or is everything new? Which do you like more?

Plan Your Travels

The easiest and cheapest way to get around Israel is still by bus. The country is small, and there are lots of buses going between cities every day.

Below is a bus schedule for buses leaving and returning to the Tel Aviv Central Bus Station. What do you want to visit today?
Use the schedule to plan out your day's travels!
You are starting your journey in Modi'in.

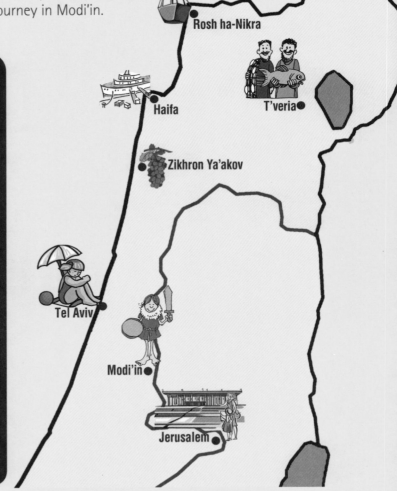

From Modi'in to Tel Aviv
6:42, 7:38, 8:17, 9:03

From Tel Aviv to Haifa
7:32, 8:04, 10:02, 11:13, 12:30, 3:03, 4:12, 4:48

From Haifa to Tel Aviv
11:19, 1:20, 3:12, 4:23, 4:51, 5:19, 6:06, 7:01

From Tel Aviv to Rosh ha–Nikra
9:12, 10:40, 12:23, 2:30, 3:59, 5:02

From Rosh ha–Nikra to Tel Aviv
10:38, 12:55, 2:45, 4:13, 5:34, 7:11

From Tel Aviv to Tiveria through Zikhron Ya'akov
7:26, 10:32, 11:43, 1:36, 2:30, 4:49, 5:32

From Tiveria to Tel Aviv through Zikhron Ya'akov
9:32, 11:42, 1:26, 2:50, 4:59, 5:52, 6:45

From Zikhron Ya'akov to Tel Aviv
10:12, 11:42, 1:16, 2:30, 4:39, 5:42, 6:55

From Tel Aviv to Modi'in
7:12, 11:42, 1:16, 4:47, 5:12, 7:55

CHAPTER 16: THE JORDAN RIVER

Joshua

Joshua was once the leader of the B'nai Yisrael. He was made their leader after the death of Moses, who led them out of slavery in Egypt.

B'nai Yisrael wandered in the desert for forty years. A whole new generation grew up in the wilderness. Finally, they reached the Land of Israel—the land that God had promised to Abraham.

THE JORDAN RiVER

On the east side of Israel is the Jordan River. This river starts in the north, and carries water between the Kinneret in the north and the Dead Sea in the south.

The Jordan is the longest river in all of Israel. When Joshua led the B'nai Yisrael into Israel, they first had to cross the Jordan River. The Bible teaches that when they got knee-deep into the river, the waters of the river stopped flowing!

Can you think of another Torah story of which this reminds you?

The Jordan River Today

Every day, lots of people spend time kayaking down the Jordan River. It's a great place to enjoy nature and play in the water. As you kayak down the river, you can see people who are camping out along the shore.

▲ Israel and Jordan use a lot of the water from the Jordan River. Many years with too little rain hasn't helped. It is a problem that Israel is working to fix.

Israel's Neighbors

Joshua and the B'nai Yisrael had to cross the Jordan River to enter the Land of Israel. The Jordan River was a boundary between Canaan (Israel before it was called Israel) and some of its neighbors.

Today, Israel still has a lot of neighbors. Some of them have good relationships with Israel. Some don't.

The area inside the green line is called the West Bank. Before the 1967 war, it was part of Jordan. Israel occupied this area and Jordan said it didn't want it back. Today there are discussions about which areas will stay part of Israel and which won't. In the 1967 war, Israel also overtook a piece of land next to Egypt called the Gaza Strip and a hilly area next to Syria called the Golan Heights.

Use another map as a resource. Fill in Israel's neighbors on this map.

53

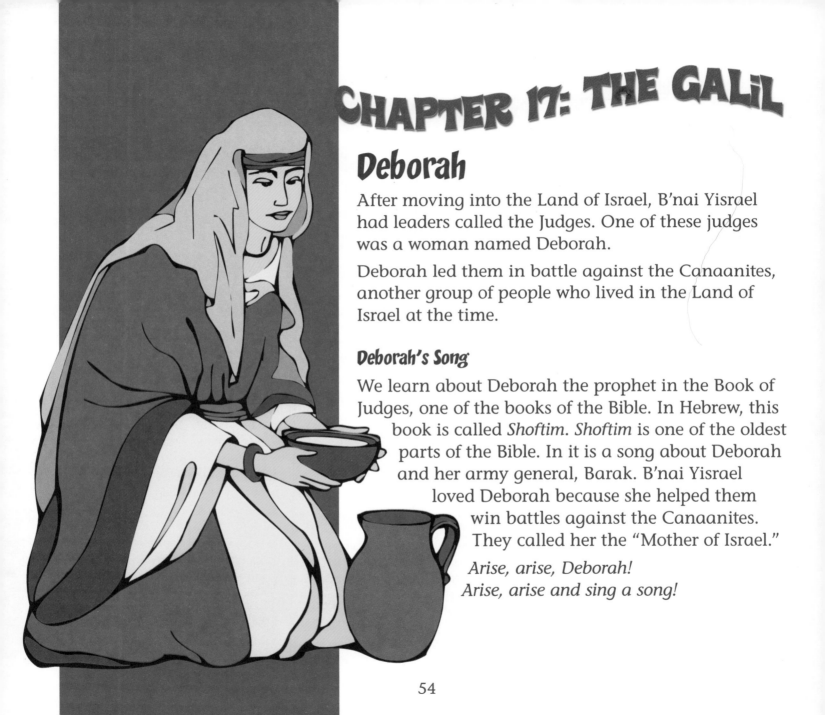

CHAPTER 17: THE GALIL

Deborah

After moving into the Land of Israel, B'nai Yisrael had leaders called the Judges. One of these judges was a woman named Deborah.

Deborah led them in battle against the Canaanites, another group of people who lived in the Land of Israel at the time.

Deborah's Song

We learn about Deborah the prophet in the Book of Judges, one of the books of the Bible. In Hebrew, this book is called *Shoftim*. *Shoftim* is one of the oldest parts of the Bible. In it is a song about Deborah and her army general, Barak. B'nai Yisrael loved Deborah because she helped them win battles against the Canaanites. They called her the "Mother of Israel."

Arise, arise, Deborah!
Arise, arise and sing a song!

HA-GALiL

The Galil (in English, the Galilee) is the northern area of Israel. It stretches south to Afula and north to the border with Lebanon. Most of northern Israel is in the Galilee.

The Galilee is known for its many rolling hills. In the south of the Galilee is the Jezreel Valley. The Galilee is one of the greenest parts of Israel and is also filled with lots of farms. The Galilee has orchards and vineyards and other types of farms as well.

When you visit the Galil, there are many things you can do. There are great hiking trails throughout the Galil. The Galil is a beautiful part of the country to walk through—the air is fresh and there are birds and trees all around.

In the Galil there are also many wineries. Visitors can go on tours to see how different Israeli wines are made!

sing a song for deborah

Deborah the prophet liked to sing. There are also lots of songs written about the Galil. A great Israeli singer-songwriter, Naomi Shemer, wrote a song called "The Eucalyptus Groves." It described one of her favorite places in the Galil.

Can you write a song about a place you love? Write a short song about a place that is special to you.

_____
_____
_____
_____
_____
_____
_____
_____

ARAB VILLAGES

There are many Arab villages in the Galilee. The Arabs who live in Israel are citizens of Israel. They vote in elections, and have their own political parties. One Israeli Arab sits on the Israeli Supreme Court. It is hard for some Arabs to live in a Jewish state. It is hard for Israel to balance being a democracy with being a Jewish state. Figuring out how to balance these two things is a challenge that Israel is constantly working on.

CHAPTER 18: TSIPORI

YEHUDAH HA-NASI

In the center of the Galilee, in the middle of a valley, is the grave of Yehudah Ha-Nasi. Just behind his grave is a big hill on the edge of the valley. At the top of that big hill is the ancient city of Tsipori.

For a time, Yehudah Ha-Nasi lived in Tsipori. Yehudah Ha-Nasi was an important person. Do you know what his name means? *Nasi* means "prince" in Hebrew. Yehudah was called a prince because, for a while, he was the head of the Jewish community. The Sanhedrin, the most important Jewish court and place of Torah, met in Tsipori at that time. Yehudah ha-Nasi was the person who put together the Mishnah, the first book of Jewish law. This became the first layer of the Talmud. In the Talmud, Yehudah Ha-Nasi is called "Rabbi."

TSiPORi

In the city's ancient buildings, archeologists have found beautiful mosaics with pictures that mix Jewish ideas and Hebrew with Roman art. When you visit Tsipori, you can see some of the mosaics still on the floors of the buildings. The synagogue there is one of the oldest synagogues in the world!

Tsipori is Hebrew for "bird." People think that the city got its name because, from Tsipori, ancient Jews had a bird's-eye view of the rest of the nearby areas. From Tsipori, you can see out to other parts of the Galil!

58

Jews and Non-Jews

Tsipori isn't just important to Jews. Lots of non-Jews have lived in Tsipori throughout history, too. At times, Jews and non-Jews lived there together. In the Talmud, there is a story about the friendship between Rabbi Yehudah ha-Nasi and the Roman governor, Antonius.

Once Antonius asked Rabbi:
"Shall I enter the world to come (heaven)?"

Rabbi said, "Yes!"

"But," said Antonius, "is it not written in your Bible, 'NONE OF THE HOUSE OF ESAU WILL SURVIVE?'" (Obadiah 1:18).

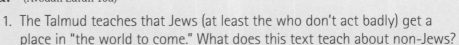

Rabbi replied, "We have been taught that 'NONE OF THE HOUSE OF ESAU WILL SURVIVE' applies only to those who act as Esau did." (Avodah Zarah 10a)

1. The Talmud teaches that Jews (at least the who don't act badly) get a place in "the world to come." What does this text teach about non-Jews?

2. What does this story teach about relationships between Jews and non-Jews?

CHAPTER 19: T'VERIA

Rabbi Moses ben Maimon was born in Cordoba, Spain. He lived almost a thousand years ago, during a time that is called the "Golden Age" of Spain. During his life, he lived all over the world—in Morocco, Egypt—and was buried in Israel. He was not just a rabbi. He was also a doctor, a scientist, and a philosopher!

Rabbi Moses ben Maimon's name is long and hard to say. Instead, we call him Rambam. "Rambam" is made by connecting together the first letters of each of the words of his Hebrew name. See if you can do it!

הָרַב מֹשֶׁה בֶּן מַימוֹן

Rabbi Moshe Ben Maimon

Rambam was a great author. He wrote books on Jewish law, philosophy, and medicine. He was the leader of a Jewish community, and was the doctor of the Grand Vizer Alfadhil, the Sultan Saladin of Egypt. There is even a rumor that he turned down an invitation to be the doctor of Richard the Lionheart of the Crusades.

Rambam is also known as Maimonides.

RABBi MOSeS BeN MAiMON

T'VERiA

Rambam is buried in the town of T'veria (Tiberias). T'veria is a city overlooking the Kinneret, in the Galilee. The whole city is built on a huge hill sloping down to the lake. From T'veria, you can see the Golan Heights to the east. T'veria is both an ancient and a modern city, just like Tzfat and Jerusalem. Jews lived in T'veria as long ago as the time of Yehudah Ha-Nasi and still do today!

T'veria has many fun things to do. There is a busy bazaar with street vendors and lots of delicious food. As you walk through the bazaar, lots of people are trying to sell you stuff, yelling out to get your attention. Sometimes, there are artists there who can write your Hebrew name on a single grain of rice!

Many visitors hang out in coffee shops or enjoy boat cruises on the Kinneret.

Rambam's Ladder of Tzedakah

Tzedakah comes from the Hebrew word צֶדֶק *tzedek*, which means justice. Tzedakah is money that you give to needy people. Rambam taught that there are different levels of tzedakah. All tzedakah is good, but some forms are even better than others. Rambam taught that the levels of giving tzedakah are like the rungs of a ladder.

There are eight different ways of giving tzedakah—each way is better than the one that comes before it.

1. The lowest way is the is the person who gives tzedakah with a frown.

2. Above this is a person who gives directly to the person in need, but gives too little, even though the tzedakah is given cheerfully.

3. The next best case is the person who gives money directly to the person in need after being asked.

4. The next best case is the person who gives money directly to the person in need before that person has to ask.

5. The next best case is one where the person who receives the tzedakah knows who has given it, but the person who is giving the tzedakah has no knowledge of the person in need.

6. The next best way of giving tzedakah is where the giver knows who will get the money, but the person who receives the tzedakah doesn't know who gave it.

7. The next best way of giving tzedakah is where the giver doesn't know who will receive the money, and the person who receives doesn't know who has given it.

8. The best way of giving is to help people help themselves by entering into a partnership or helping them find a job.

No matter how it is given, giving tzedakah is a mitzvah.

1. Why is the first way of giving (number 1) the worst way?
2. Why is the last way of giving (number 8) the best way?
3. What other tzedakah rules would you add?

CHAPTER 20: KIBBUTZIM

Berl Katznelson

Berl Katznelson was a small man with messy hair. But he had a very big impact on Israel. Berl cared a lot about the Jewish people. He wanted to help Jews move to the Land of Israel. He didn't like the fact that not many Jews knew how to be farmers or work the land. He believed that part of the dream of Zionism was for Jews to reconnect with the land.

He was part of a group of people called Labor Zionists. They were very important in helping to build modern Israel. Katznelson believed that Jewish workers could make Israel a great country. He believed that working hard with your own hands to build something was a great thing. He thought it was even holy.

He said, "Everywhere the Jewish laborer goes, the Divine Presence goes, too."

Have you ever worked really hard to build something? How did it make you feel? Were you proud of what you did?

KIBBUTZ

One of the ways that Berl Katznelson thought Jews could work together was by living side by side on kibbutzim. A kibbutz is a small village with farms and homes where a group of Jews live and work together. On a kibbutz, everyone is equal and everything is communal.

That means that no one is special and no one owns anything. Everything belongs to the whole kibbutz. The kibbutzniks work hard in their farms or factories, and make money for the kibbutz. Then, the kibbutz makes sure that kibbutzniks have everything they need, like a home, food, and medicine.

You don't need to be a member of a kibbutz to visit one. Many kibbutzim have guesthouses. You can stay there at night, and then go visit other places in the country during the day. Some kibbutzim have summer programs so teenagers and young adults can come and learn Hebrew. You can spend time working the fields of kibbutzim, too! Just like the early *kibbutznikim*, you can pick fruit in the orchard, and milk the cows.

Ulpan Time

Lots of people go to kibbutzim to take part in an ulpan. An ulpan is a program where people come together to learn to speak Hebrew. All day long, you study and speak in Hebrew until you are fluent!

It's time for you to learn Hebrew. Below are some important Hebrew words. Connect them with their meanings in English!

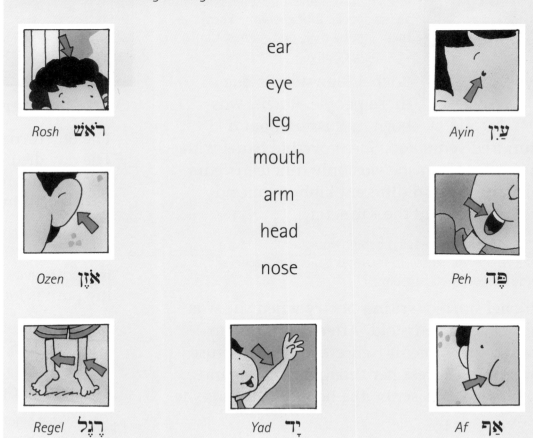

Rosh רֹאשׁ

Ozen אֹזֶן

Regel רֶגֶל

ear

eye

leg

mouth

arm

head

nose

Yad יָד

Ayin עַיִן

Peh פֶּה

Af אַף

CHAPTER 21: THE KINNERET

Rachel

Almost everyone these days has a first and last name. But some people are so special that everyone knows them just by their first names. Can you think of any?

Rachel Bluwstein is one of those people. Rachel was born in Russia about a hundred years ago. She moved to Israel with her sister when she was only nineteen years old. She lived in different kibbutzim and villages around the Kinneret.

Can you imagine leaving behind your family and everything you know to move to Israel like Rachel did? Why do you think she did it?

Rachel started writing poetry when she was only fifteen years old. After she moved to Israel, she wrote in Hebrew. She liked to use poetry to express her thoughts and feelings. She wrote to describe the beautiful things she saw.

One of her poems is called "Mood."

The day turned into night,
The day died.
The sky and mountains
were plated in gold.

Around me the field was black
silent field;
my path goes on—my path is lonely
my path is lonesome.

But I shall not escape my fate
crushing fate,
Happy I will go on,
Thankful for everything.

1. What emotions does Rachel express?
2. How does this poem make you feel?

KINNERET

To Rachel, the Kinneret was one of the most beautiful parts of all of Israel.

The Kinneret is a lake in the north of Israel, in the Galilee. It is surrounded by lots of small kibbutzim, like the ones that Rachel lived on, as well as by T'veria, where Rambam is buried. The area is very green with lots of plants.

Israelis love to come to the Kinneret for vacations. They relax on the shore of the lake, and play in the water. You can go for cruises on the lake at night. There is even a water park on the shore of the Kinneret!

The Kinneret is the only big body of fresh water in Israel. Because Israel gets so little rain, that means that the Kinneret is very important. It is not just a beautiful place—Israelis depend on the Kinneret to live. Sometimes, when the water level of the Kinneret gets too low, Israelis have to work hard to save water and not waste even a drop.

Rachel is buried on the shore of the Kinneret. Whenever someone goes to visit her grave, they can enjoy the beauty of the Kinneret and the whole Galilee—just what she loved! Think of a place that is special to you. What is your most favorite place in the world? Is it inside or outside? Is it in the city or in nature? Write your own poem.

Use this space to write a poem about a place that is special to you.

CHAPTER 22: TZFAT

RABBI ISAAC LURIA

Rabbi Isaac Luria came to Tzfat around the time of Christopher Columbus. He was part of a generation of Jews who had to flee Spain. Some went north to places like Amsterdam. Others went south to Africa. Some, like Isaac Luria, came to Israel.

Isaac Luria was a great Kabbalist. Kabbalah is Jewish mysticism. It is a way to think about how the world was created, what God is really like, and what may happen to us after we die. Rabbi Luria taught his students new ideas. He told the following story:

When God created the world, sparks of holiness—little pieces of God—went flying throughout the entire world. We don't know where these sparks are. They can be in your synagogue, or in the forest, or in the love between you and your parents.

It is the job of every person to find the sparks of God and bring them back together by doing good deeds, and justice, and helping others out. This is called *Tikkun Olam*. It means "repairing the world."

Have you helped out your parents with chores, or given food to homeless people? Have you been polite in school or helped a friend with homework? All these things are a part of making the world a better place.

TZFAT

Tzfat is a small city on the top of a huge mountain in the north of the Galilee. It is one of the few places in Israel where it snows in the winter. Not many people live in Tzfat, but it has been a very important place to Jews for a long time. That has a lot to do with Isaac Luria.

When you visit Tzfat, you can see Isaac Luria's synagogue. It still stands to this day! In another part of the city, there is a long alley between the small stone buildings. On both sides of the alley, artists sell their pictures and paintings and Jewish objects. The artist's colony is a fun place to shop for beautiful art.

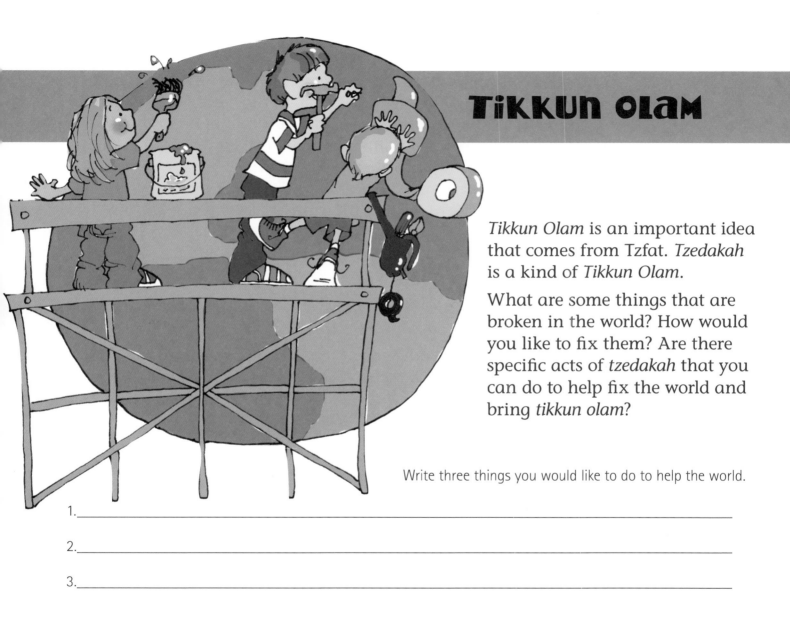

TiKKun OLaM

Tikkun Olam is an important idea that comes from Tzfat. *Tzedakah* is a kind of *Tikkun Olam*.

What are some things that are broken in the world? How would you like to fix them? Are there specific acts of *tzedakah* that you can do to help fix the world and bring *tikkun olam*?

Write three things you would like to do to help the world.

1._____

2._____

3._____

Elijah

Elijah the prophet lived after King Solomon. Elijah lived up in the north of Israel, in the Galil. One thing that was important to Elijah was to fight against those who worshipped different gods. The king of Israel at the time, Ahab, along with his wife Jezebel, worshipped a god named Ba'al. Many of B'nai Yisrael worshipped Ba'al, too. Elijah wanted them to worship The One God again.

On Mount Carmel, in the north of Israel, Elijah defeated the priests of Ba'al.

There are many times when we remember Elijah the prophet. Can you think of any?

- At the end of Shabbat, Havdalah marks the beginning of the week. At the end of the Havdalah service, we sing *Eliahu ha-Navi*, Elijah the Prophet, to remember him.

- On Passover, we set aside a special cup of wine for Elijah. Towards the end of the Seder we open the door to welcome Elijah into our home.

- At the ceremony that welcomes a newborn Jewish child, Elijah is a guest.

Elijah is a symbol of the future hopes of the Jewish people. There are many folk tales about Elijah visiting people and rewarding their good deeds.

HAiFA

Today, on Mount Carmel, there is the beautiful city of <u>H</u>aifa. It is very green and has lots of trees. It also has beautiful beaches with white sand.

There are three parts to the city: the base of Mount Carmel, called *namal* (port); *Hadar ha-Carmel*, (the slope of Mount Carmel); and *Har ha-Carmel* (the top of Mount Carmel).

<u>H</u>aifa has a port. Lots of products shipped to Israel come through <u>H</u>aifa. There are huge cranes which lift shipping containers out of ships and into the port. Lots of big ships, even aircraft carriers, dock in the Haifa port.

73

On the side of Mount Carmel are the Baha'i Gardens. They are beautiful to walk through. In the center of the gardens is the Baha'i Temple. Haifa is the world center of the Baha'i religion. Baha'is believe in the unity of all religions. They believe that religious leaders like Moses, Jesus, Mohammed, and Buddha are all messengers of God.

On top of Mount Carmel are lots of residential neighborhoods as well as two important universities: Haifa University and the Technion.

The Druze

Near to Haifa are a series of Druze villages. The Druze are their own group. They have a secret religion and are good friends to Israel. They have their own schools and their own culture. They serve in the Israeli army.

Send a Postcard Home!

Now that you've had a chance to learn about different parts of <u>H</u>aifa, it's time to send a postcard home from Israel's northern port city. On the postcard below, fill out a short letter to your family and friends about your favorite things to do in <u>H</u>aifa.

CHAPTER 24: ZIKHRON YA'AKOV

Baron Edmond James de Rothschild

Just inland from the coast, near <u>H</u>aifa, is a small town on top of a hill. From there you can see the Mediterranean Sea. The town's name is Zikhron Ya'akov. What does the name mean? Can you see any words you know? Zikhron Ya'akov means "remembering Jacob." So who was Jacob?

The town was one of the first modern settlements in Israel. It was helped by Baron Edmond James de Rothschild. Jacob was his father. Baron Rothschild was a very wealthy man from France who lived more than a hundred years ago. He gave money to Jews who wanted to move back to the Land of Israel. He helped them to become farmers and turned Zikhron Ya'akov into an agricultural village. He also built a large synagogue in the center of the town.

Living in Israel at the time was not easy. The weather was hot, and settlers didn't have things like air conditioning or cars. They had to spend the whole day doing really hard work in the fields. There was also the danger of getting sick. Lots of the people died. Many others gave up. But some didn't, and continued to work to make Zikhron Ya'akov succeed. The pioneers built a big winery that still exists today!

ZiKHRON YA'AKOV

Zikhron Ya'akov is a place for vacations and tourists. It was a small farming village established in 1882 by a group of idealistic Romanian immigrants. Its main street still looks the same as it did back then. When you visit Zikhron Ya'akov, you can sit in restaurants on the same main street built by those original pioneers and Baron Rothschild more than a hundred years ago. There are lots of boutiques and crafts stores to shop in. You can still visit the synagogue built there during Baron Rothschild's time. Today, the winery remains in action, as do the huge wine cellars that were carved into the mountain over a century ago.

Zikhron Ya'akov has beautiful views and wonderful gardens. It has clean air and you can see the Mediterranean Sea.

▼ To make wine the old fashioned way, you crush grapes by stepping on them.

Klal Yisrael

Why did Baron Rothschild give so much time and money to help the pioneers of the Land of Israel build towns and farms?

One important Jewish value is *klal Yisrael*, which means "all of Israel." Even though we may live very far from each other and speak different languages, all Jews are connected to each other. We share the same history, hopes, and Hebrew! Every Jew should do what they can to help other Jews in need.

Baron Rothschild showed us an example of the value of *klal Yisrael* by helping out the pioneers of Zikhron Ya'akov. If it weren't for him, they may not have succeeded.

What are some ways that you can help out Jews around the world? How can you bring the value of *klal Yisrael* into your life? Make a list below of three ways that you can help other Jews in need. Then, make another list of ways that other Jews have helped you!

Things You Can Do For Other Jews	Things Other Jews Have Done For You
1. _____	1. _____
2. _____	2. _____
3. _____	3. _____

CHAPTER 25: TEL AVIV

Menahem Sheinkin

Menahem Sheinkin was one of the founders of Tel Aviv. Sheinkin was an activist in the _Hovavei Tzion_ (Lovers of Zion) organization. He was one of the creators of the Herzeliya Gymnasia, the first Hebrew high school in Israel. And he was the person who first suggested the name for Tel Aviv.

What does the name Tel Aviv mean? The words "Tel Aviv" are mentioned in the Bible in Ezekiel 3:15. In Israel, there are lots of sites where the remains of one ancient city are right on top of the remains of an even older one. Over time, new cities are built and then are destroyed, and new ones rise. This creates a small hill deep in history. This kind of hill is a _tel_. _Aviv_ is the Hebrew word for spring. So while _Tel_ has a meaning of "old," _Aviv_ has a meaning of "new". This is just what Tel Aviv is—a mix of the old and new, right on the beautiful coast of Israel!

TEL AVIV

Tel Aviv may have been a bunch of sand dunes, but it has much more than just sand now! Tel Aviv is a huge city, with skyscrapers, malls, hotels, and office buildings. There are lots of museums in Tel Aviv where you can see modern art and old art, or learn about Jewish communities from around the world. In the center of town is *Ha-Bimah*. *Bimah* means stage. It is the word we use to describe the raised platform in a synagogue. In Tel Aviv, *Ha-Bimah* is Israel's national theater. There are performances there all year long.

By far, one of the most popular attractions of Tel Aviv is the beach. Along the beach is a long promenade, called the *tayelet*. People walk up and down the *tayelet* day and night. You can sit on benches and talk with friends, or just appreciate the beautiful beach next to you. The beach is filled with soft, white sand.

People spend all day lying in the sun, swimming in the waves, or playing games with friends. There are even restaurants by the beach, where people come to have fun and enjoy everything that Tel Aviv has to offer.

Build It from Scratch

Tel Aviv was the first modern Israeli city. It was built from scratch on a bunch of sand dunes.

If you were designing your own Israeli city from scratch, what are some things you would build. What would you want your city to look like? What would make it special?

Use the space below to either draw a picture of your Israeli city, or write about it.

MEIR DIZENGOFF

Meir Dizengoff was one of the first people to move to the new city of Tel Aviv. He and his wife Zina owned a huge house on Rothschild Street in Tel Aviv. Rothschild Street is a large boulevard in Tel Aviv, with a park down the middle.

When Meir Dizengoff and his wife died, they left their house to the city of Tel Aviv to make into an art museum. The Dizengoffs loved art, and wanted to make sure that other Tel Avivians would have a museum where they could enjoy artwork.

The house became a very important museum, unlike almost any other in the whole world.

CHAPTER 26: INDEPENDENCE HALL

INDEPENDENCE HALL

On May 14, 1948, it was time to declare independence for the new country. It was a Friday afternoon, and Israel's leaders needed to gather before the start of Shabbat. They chose Meir Dizengoff's home as their meeting place.

The main room was cleaned up and filled with chairs for everyone to sit in. Two large Israeli flags were hung. The leaders read the Declaration of Independence. This made Israel a country for the first time in almost two thousand years.

Israelis filled the streets to dance, sing, and celebrate their new independence! We still celebrate that day every year in the spring on *Yom ha-Atzmaut* (Israeli Independence Day).

Today, the museum created from Meir Dizengoff's house tells the story of how Israel gained its independence. As you enter the building, you see the main room still set up just as it was on May 14, 1948. There is a copy of the Declaration of Independence and a recording of David Ben Gurion reading it aloud.

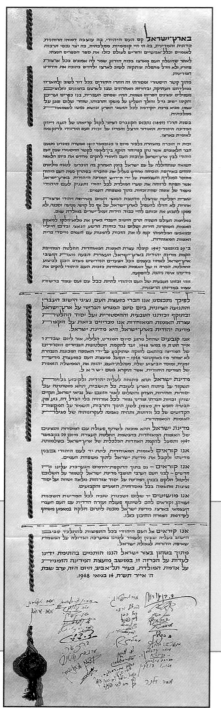

HA-TiKVAH

Israel's national anthem is called *Ha-Tikvah*. *Tikvah* is the Hebrew word meaning hope. Hope is what allowed Jews to create Israel after two thousand years without a country. Hope is what helped us to survive through some of the more difficult parts of history. Hope is one of the things that makes Israel the great place it is today.

To the left is a picture of the Declaration of Independence. Here is part of the last paragraph of the declaration.

Eretz Yisrael was the birthplace of the Jewish people. Here their spiritual, religious and political identity was shaped. Here they first attained statehood, created cultural values of national and universal significance, and gave to the world the eternal Book of Books...by virtue of our natural and historic right and on the strength of the resolution of the United Nations general assembly, hereby declare the establishment of a Jewish State in Eretz-Israel, to be known as the State of Israel.

Imagine yourself at Independence Hall on the night this declaration was signed. Add your own signature to show your support for the State of Israel.

DiZENGOFF CENTER

In the middle of Tel Aviv is a big city center named after Zina Dizengoff. Dizengoff Center has two parts. Outside is a big plaza with a colorful fountain in the center. Lots of times throughout the year, Israelis gather here for protests. Israelis love to protest! They protest about politics and religion and anything about which they have a strong opinion.

Inside Dizengoff Center is a big mall and shopping center. There are restaurants and clothing stores. Israelis gather here day and night to meet with friends, go shopping, and have fun. Dizengoff Center is a fun place to hang out after a busy day of touring Tel Aviv.

In 1992, Yitzhak Rabin was elected to be the prime minister of Israel. He had spent most of his life as a soldier and as a military leader. He wanted nothing more than to bring peace to Israel. He tried as hard as he could to make peace with Israel's Arab neighbors. He offered to give land in exchange for peace.

Lots of Israelis supported his efforts. Jews around the world were excited by the possibility of peace finally coming to Israel after so many years of war. On November 4, 1995, thousands of Israelis gathered in a big square in the center of Tel Aviv to show their support for peace. They waved flags, heard speeches, and sang songs.

Not all Israelis liked what Yitzhak Rabin was doing. On the night of that big rally, one Israeli tried to stop Yitzhak Rabin from making peace with the Arabs. His name was Yigal Amir. As Yitzhak Rabin was leaving the rally, Yigal Amir shot him in the chest. Yitzhak Rabin died that night.

At his funeral, leaders from all around the world came to pay their respects to Yitzhak Rabin. President Bill Clinton even spoke at the funeral. At the end of his speech he said, "Shalom haver," "Goodbye friend."

KIKAR RABIN

The square where Yitzhak Rabin was killed is in the middle of downtown Tel Aviv. It is now named Kikar Rabin, which means "Rabin Square." There is a big memorial to Yitzhak Rabin on the spot where he was killed.

People come to visit Kikar Rabin to pay respect to the fallen leader. They learn the history of his life and how he was killed.

Kikar Rabin is next to the municipal building of Tel Aviv. The municipal building is where all of the city's important business gets done.

Kikar Rabin is surrounded by some of the busiest parts of downtown Tel Aviv. Across the street from Kikar Rabin is one of the best falafel stands in Tel Aviv. They make their pita fresh when you order it! There are lots of shops and restaurants and even an American coffee shop in the area!

Graffiti

On the walls around the memorial, there is a lot of graffiti that people scribbled after Rabin's death. Some people wrote about how sad they were, others wrote *"Shalom, haver"*.

Draw your own graffiti in tribute to Yitzhak Rabin. How will you help to remember this Jewish hero?

Evan grew up near Atlanta, Georgia. As a kid, he went to Hebrew school, liked sports, and liked to hang out with his friends. Evan fell in love with Israel the first time he visited. When he was a teenager, he came on a trip and spent the summer in the country. As soon as he got to Israel, Evan felt like he was home.

Evan loved seeing signs in Hebrew. They reminded him of his synagogue, the Jewish holidays, and Hebrew school. Evan loved walking down the street and seeing lots of different types of Jews. Some wore *kippot*, while others had bare heads. They were all so different, but all of them were Jewish!

Evan loved smelling the <u>h</u>allot being sold in stores on Fridays. The smells reminded him of being in the kitchen with his family.

What are some things that you love about Israel?

A few years ago, Evan decided to make *aliyah*. He picked up and moved to Israel. Evan now lives in an apartment in downtown Tel Aviv. For a while, he spent time in an ulpan. Ulpan is where some people new to Israel learn Hebrew. Ulpan was very hard for Evan, but now he is much better at speaking Hebrew!

REHOV SHEINKIN

One place Evan loves to visit is Sheinkin Street. Sheinkin Street is in the heart of downtown Tel Aviv. It is named after Menahem Sheinkin, the same man who came up with the name "Tel Aviv." Many young people come to Sheinkin Street to shop and eat. There are cool stores to browse in and, of course, falafel stands.

You can walk down Sheinkin Street and shop, talk with friends, or just have fun. In the middle of Sheinkin Street is a park where people bring their dogs for walks. People sit in the coffee shops on Sheinkin and talk politics or catch up with old friends all day long.

Across the street is the Nahalat Binyamin marketplace. Two days a week, the outdoor market is filled with artists selling arts and crafts. Nahalat Binyamin is a great place to buy Jewish objects, like mezuzot. Connected to Nahalat Binyamin is the Carmel Market, where you can buy cheap groceries and even clothing.

Evan loves to come to Sheinkin Street on Friday mornings to have breakfast, and then shop on Nahalat Binyamin before Shabbat.

SOCCER!

In Israel soccer is called football. Evan loves to go to football games in Israel. Tel Aviv's football team is Ha-Poel Tel Aviv. Evan goes there to watch games all the time.

Going to a football game in Israel is a lot like going to an American football game except for a few differences. Look at the picture of this game in Israel. Circle the things that are different from what you're used to seeing in an American football game. What is different?

ENDINGS

The story of Israel started with Abraham, the first Jew. And along the way, Israel's story has included heroes and poets, farmers and politicians, students and rabbis.

Deborah defended Israel from its enemies in the Galilee. Eliezer ben Yehudah helped to create modern Hebrew in Jerusalem. Isaac Luria taught about mysticism in Tzfat. The poet Rachel worked on kibbutzim by the Kinneret.

There is no end to Israel's story. It continues today!

How do you want to be a part of Israel's story? How will you bring Israel's story into your own life and family?

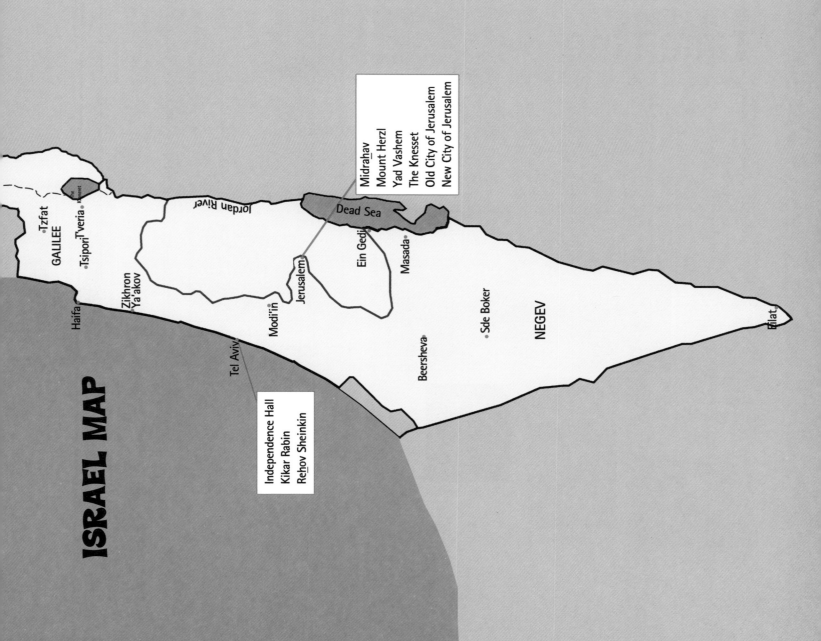

ISRAEL MAP

Midrahav
Mount Herzl
Yad Vashem
The Knesset
Old City of Jerusalem
New City of Jerusalem

Independence Hall
Kikar Rabin
Rehov Sheinkin

Dead Sea

Jordan River

Kinneret

Izfat

GALILEE

Tsipori Tveria

Zikhron
Ya'akov

Haifa

Tel Aviv

Modi'in

Jerusalem

Ein Gedi

Masada

Beersheva

Sde Boker

NEGEV

Eilat

Time Line

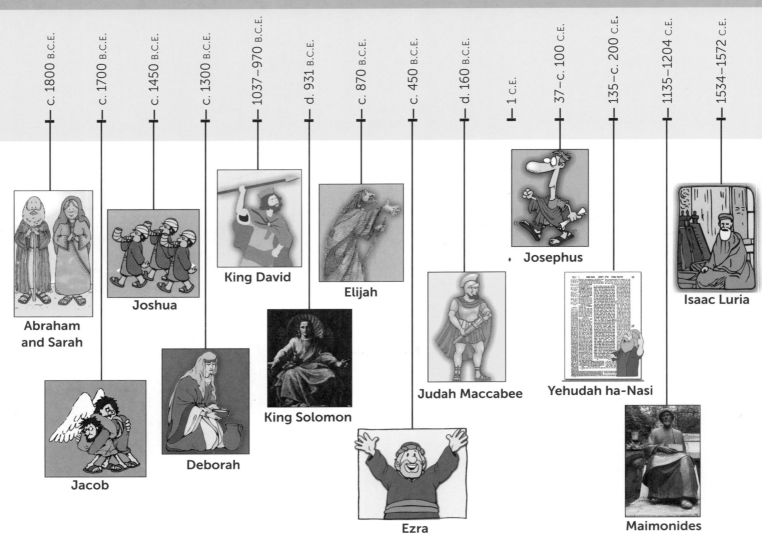

c. 1800 B.C.E. — Abraham and Sarah

c. 1700 B.C.E. — Jacob

c. 1450 B.C.E. — Joshua

c. 1300 B.C.E. — Deborah

1037–970 B.C.E. — King David / King Solomon

d. 931 B.C.E. — Elijah

c. 870 B.C.E. — Elijah

c. 450 B.C.E. — Ezra

d. 160 B.C.E. — Judah Maccabee

1 C.E. — Josephus

37–c. 100 C.E. — Josephus

135–c. 200 C.E. — Yehudah ha-Nasi

1135–1204 C.E. — Maimonides

1534–1572 C.E. — Isaac Luria

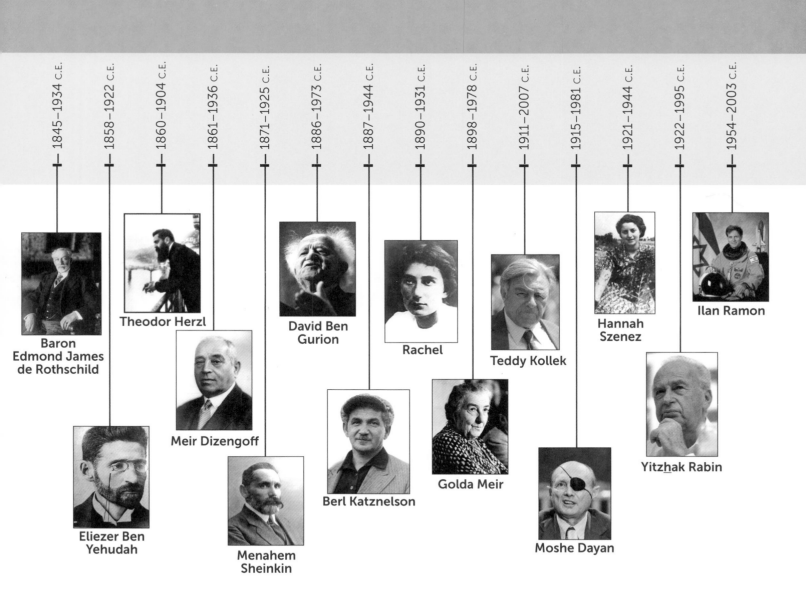

1845–1934 C.E.

1858–1922 C.E.

1860–1904 C.E.

1861–1936 C.E.

1871–1925 C.E.

1886–1973 C.E.

1887–1944 C.E.

1890–1931 C.E.

1898–1978 C.E.

1911–2007 C.E.

1915–1981 C.E.

1921–1944 C.E.

1922–1995 C.E.

1954–2003 C.E.

Baron
Edmond James
de Rothschild

Theodor Herzl

Eliezer Ben
Yehudah

Meir Dizengoff

Menahem
Sheinkin

David Ben
Gurion

Berl Katznelson

Rachel

Golda Meir

Teddy Kollek

Moshe Dayan

Hannah
Szenez

Yitzhak Rabin

Ilan Ramon